Friends for Baby in Plastic Canvas

THERE'S A NEW KID ON THE WAY!

Surprise the mom-to-be with these bears, ducks, bunnies, and other cute characters—all stitched on plastic canvas! You'll find an adorable set of shower favors and a clown bear basket that's perfect for your party centerpiece. For gifts, it's fun to make tissue box covers and little photo frames. There are even bear-themed items to brighten the nursery with a necessities box, switch plate cover, and wall decoration. It's time to get stitching for a special baby who's going to love seeing these sweet creations.

TABLE OF CONTENTS

ABOUT THE DESIGNER

These cheery projects are among the thousands created by the late Dick Martin, a genial and imaginative designer whose friendship we treasured and whose publications are a valued part of the Leisure Arts library. We are pleased to present this sampling of his designs so that you can create these thoughtful gifts in plastic canvas.

LEISURE ARTS, INC.
Little Rock, Arkansas

Small Fry Frames

Duck

Size
8"w x 6"h

Supplies
One 10½" x 13½" sheet
of 7 mesh plastic canvas
Worsted weight yarn
#16 tapestry needle
³/₁₆" dia dowel

Stitches Used
Backstitch, Cross Stitch, French Knot, Gobelin Stitch, Overcast Stitch, and Tent Stitch. Refer to **General Instructions**, pages 36-39, for stitch diagrams.

Instructions
Follow charts to cut and stitch, overcasting only where indicated on charts. Matching ●'s, use orange to join unworked edges of Beaks to Body, working through all thicknesses. Matching ♦'s and □'s, use yellow to join Wing to Body along unworked edges. With Frame Front behind Body, match ☆'s and △'s. Using color to match stitching area of Body, join Frame Front to Body. Tack one Leaf and one Flower at each ✖. Insert a 3½" length of ³/₁₆" dia dowel under stitches on back of Large Cattail with 3" extending below cattail. Insert a 2½" length of ³/₁₆" dia dowel under stitches on back of Small Cattail with 2" extending below cattail. Using green, attach Large Cattail at ▲ and Small Cattail at ◖. Matching ♦'s, use green to attach each Cattail Leaf to Body at ♦'s. Follow **Frame Finishing**, page 7, to complete frame.

Color Key	
▨	yellow
▨	orange
▨	pink
▨	lt blue
▨	green
▨	brown
▟	black
⦿	orange Fr. Knot

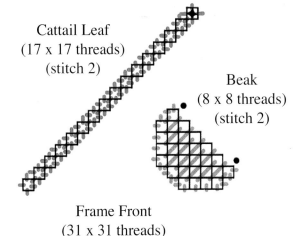

Cattail Leaf
(17 x 17 threads)
(stitch 2)

Beak
(8 x 8 threads)
(stitch 2)

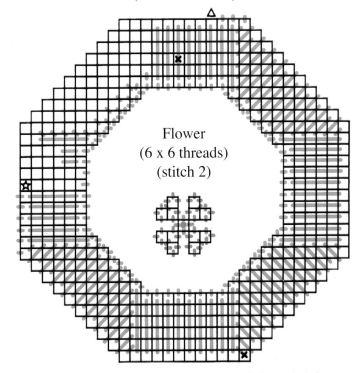

Frame Front
(31 x 31 threads)

Flower
(6 x 6 threads)
(stitch 2)

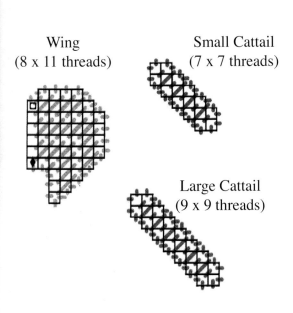

Wing
(8 x 11 threads)

Small Cattail
(7 x 7 threads)

Large Cattail
(9 x 9 threads)

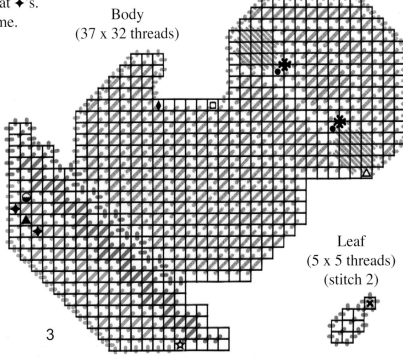

Body
(37 x 32 threads)

Leaf
(5 x 5 threads)
(stitch 2)

Bunny

Shown on page 2.

Size

8"w x 7¼"h

Supplies

One 10½" x 13½" sheet of 7 mesh plastic canvas
Worsted weight yarn
#16 tapestry needle

Stitches Used

Backstitch, Cross Stitch, French Knot, Gobelin Stitch, Overcast Stitch, and Tent Stitch. Refer to **General Instructions**, pages 36-39, for stitch diagrams.

Instructions

Follow charts to cut and stitch, overcasting only where indicated on charts. Matching △'s, use white to attach Carrot behind Arm. Matching ★'s and **S**'s, use pink to join Arm to Body along unworked edges. With Frame Front behind Body, match ●'s and ♦'s. Using color to match stitching area of Body, join Frame Front to Body. Tack one Leaf and one Flower at each ✳. Thread 8" of green yarn through Carrot at ▲; tie a bow and trim ends. Follow **Frame Finishing**, page 7, to complete frame.

Color Key

▨ white		▨ green	
▨ lt pink		▨ tan	
▨ pink		▨ black	
▨ orange		⊙ orange Fr. Knot	

Flower (6 x 6 threads)
(stitch 2)

Arm (10 x 9 threads)

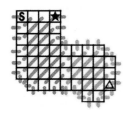

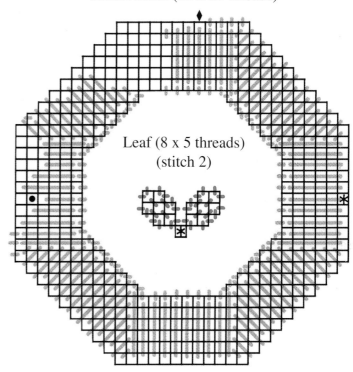

Frame Front (31 x 31 threads)

Leaf (8 x 5 threads)
(stitch 2)

Carrot (9 x 9 threads)

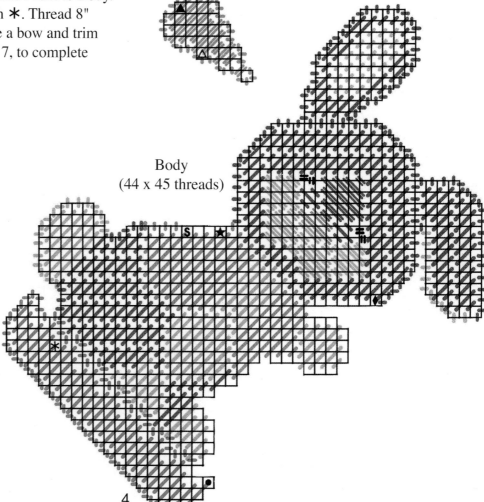

Body
(44 x 45 threads)

4

Bear

Shown on page 2.

Size

8"w x 5³/₄"h

Supplies

One 10¹/₂" x 13¹/₂" sheet of 7 mesh plastic canvas
Worsted weight yarn
#16 tapestry needle

Stitches Used

Backstitch, Cross Stitch, French Knot, Gobelin Stitch, Overcast Stitch, and Tent Stitch. Refer to **General Instructions**, pages 36-39, for stitch diagrams.

Instructions

Follow charts to cut and stitch, overcasting only where indicated on charts. Matching ✚'s, use blue to join Right Arm to Body along unworked edges. Matching ♦'s, use blue to join Left Arm to Body along unworked edges. Matching ▲'s and ■'s, use tan to join Leg to Body. Tie 10" of blue yarn in a bow around neck; trim ends. With Frame Front behind Body, match △'s and ◔'s. Using color to match stitching area of Body, join Frame Front to Body. Tack one Small Flower at each ☐. Tack Small Leaf and one Large Flower at ✱. Tack Medium Leaf and one Large Flower at **S**. Tack Large Leaf and one Large Flower at ◊. Follow **Frame Finishing**, page 7, to complete frame.

Medium Leaf
(8 x 5 threads)

Large Flower
(6 x 6 threads)
(stitch 3)

Frame Front (31 x 31 threads)

Small Flower
(4 x 4 threads)
(stitch 2)

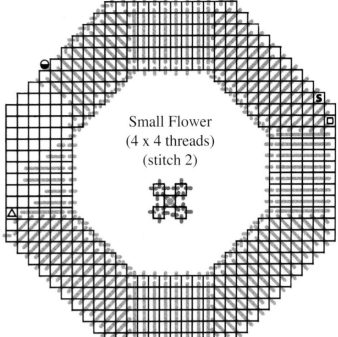

Left Arm (11 x 6 threads)

Right Arm (12 x 6 threads)

Body
(42 x 43 threads)

Leg
(15 x 15 threads)

Small Leaf
(5 x 5 threads)

Large Leaf
(10 x 6 threads)

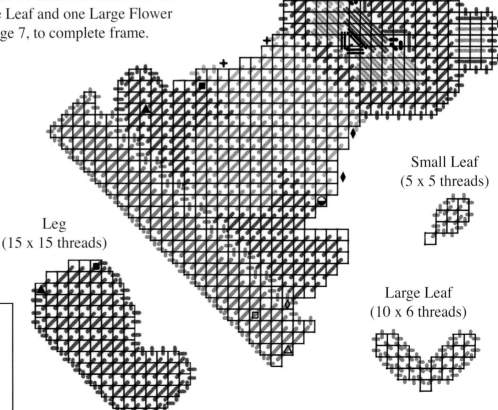

Color Key

▨ white		▨ blue	
▨ lt pink		▨ green	
▨ pink		▨ lt tan	
▨ orange		▨ tan	
▨ purple		◣ black	
		◉ orange Fr. Knot	

5

Kitten

Shown on page 2.

Size

7¹/₈"w x 5⁵/₈"h

Supplies

One 10¹/₂" x 13¹/₂" sheet of 7 mesh plastic canvas
Worsted weight yarn
#16 tapestry needle

Stitches Used

Backstitch, Cross Stitch, Gobelin Stitch, Overcast
Stitch, and Tent Stitch. Refer to **General Instructions**,
pages 36-39, for stitch diagrams.

Instructions

Follow charts to cut and stitch, overcasting only where
indicated on charts. Matching ▲'s, use blue to join
Bow to Body along unworked edges. Matching ✖'s,
use lt grey to join Right Arm to Body along unworked
edges. Matching ♦'s, use lt grey to join Left Arm to
Body along unworked edges. Matching ♦'s and ☆'s,
use lt grey to join Tail to Body along unworked edges.
Matching ✳'s, use pink to attach Yarn Ball to Body.
With Frame Front behind Body, match ★'s and ☐'s.
Using color to match stitching area of Body, join Frame
Front to Body. Using 15" of pink yarn, secure yarn
and come up at ✳. Referring to photo, wrap around
Arms and thread end back through canvas at △. Follow
Frame Finishing, page 7, to complete frame.

Frame Front
(31 x 31 threads)

Bow
(7 x 7 threads)

Color Key

▱	white
▱	lt yellow
▱	pink
▱	blue
▱	green
▱	lt grey
▰	grey
▰	black

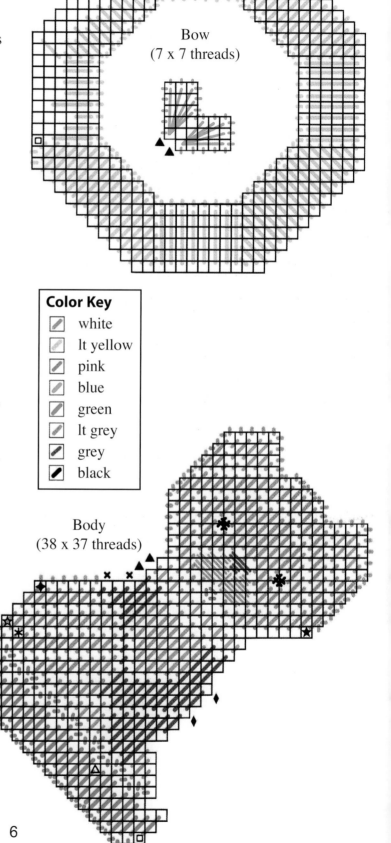

Body
(38 x 37 threads)

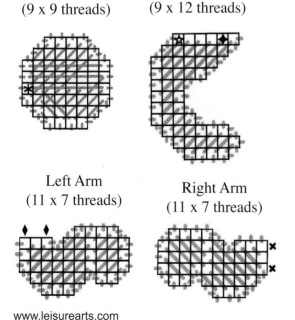

Yarn Ball
(9 x 9 threads)

Tail
(9 x 12 threads)

Left Arm
(11 x 7 threads)

Right Arm
(11 x 7 threads)

Frame Finishing

Instructions

Overcast where indicated on chart using color to match Frame Front. Depending on how Frame will be displayed, join either Stand or Hanger to Frame Back. Using color to match Frame Front, join Frame Back to Frame Front along unworked edges.

Stand: Use color to match Frame Front for all joining. Matching ●'s, join Stand Back to Stand Bottom between ●'s. Matching ★'s, join Stand Back to Frame Back between ★'s. Matching ■'s, join Stand Bottom to Frame Back between ■'s.

Frame Back (31 x 31 threads)

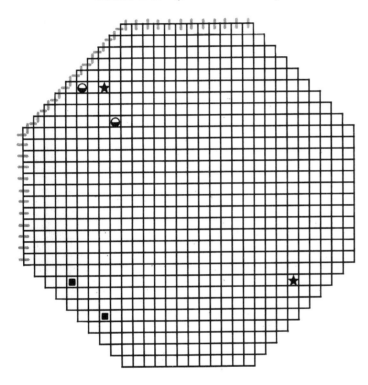

Stand Back (31 x 31 threads)

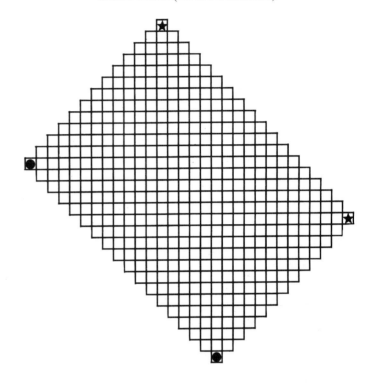

Hanger: Use color to match Frame Front for all joining. Matching ◒'s, join Hanger to Frame Back between ◒'s.

Hanger (8 x 8 threads)

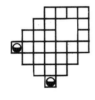

Stand Bottom (21 x 21 threads)

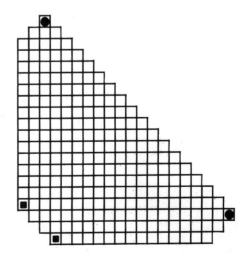

7

Baby Boutiques

Giraffe

Size

5"w x 15½"h x 6½"d
(fits a 4¼"w x 5¼"h x 4¼"d boutique tissue box)

Supplies

Three 10½" x 13½" sheets of 7 mesh
plastic canvas
Worsted weight yarn
#16 tapestry needle

Stitches Used

Backstitch, Diagonal Mosaic Stitch, French Knot,
Gobelin Stitch, Overcast Stitch, Scotch Stitch, and Tent
Stitch. Refer to **General Instructions**, pages 36-39, for
stitch diagrams.

Color Key

🖊	lt yellow
🖊	green
🖊	lavender
⦿	pink Fr. Knot

Instructions

Follow charts to cut and stitch pieces. Refer to Diagram
B, page 10, to assemble pieces. Matching ♥'s, use
lt yellow to join Head Center to Neck Center. Using
matching color Overcast Stitches, match ▲'s to join
center pieces to Head and Neck Side #1. Match ✱'s
to join center pieces to Head and Neck Side #2. Using
lt yellow Overcast Stitches, cover unworked edges of
Head and Neck Sides, Neck Center, and Head Center.

Referring to Diagram A for stitch pattern, join Top to
Sides. Matching ♦'s, use lt yellow yarn to tack bottom
edges of Head and Neck Sides to Top. Match ★'s to
tack Neck Center to Top and one Side through three
thicknesses of canvas.

Using lt yellow Overcast Stitches, cover unworked edges
of Ear pieces. Using lt yellow yarn, refer to photo for
placement and tack Ears to Head and Neck Sides. Using
matching color Overcast Stitches, join Sides together
along long edges. Cover unworked edges of Sides.

Using pink Overcast Stitches, cover unworked edges
of Flowers. Using lt yellow yarn, refer to photo for
placement and tack one Flower to each Side. Tack
remaining Flower to neck. Cut two 20" lengths of pink
yarn and knot ends together; tie a bow around neck.

Top (44 x 44 threads)

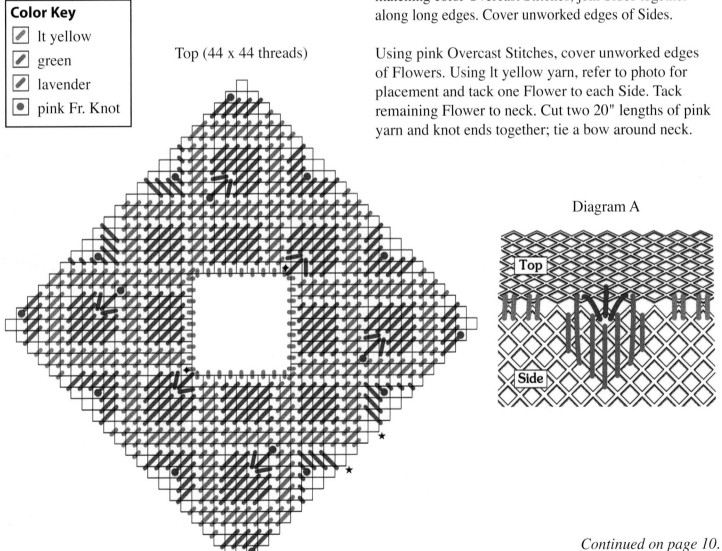

Diagram A

Continued on page 10.

Diagram B

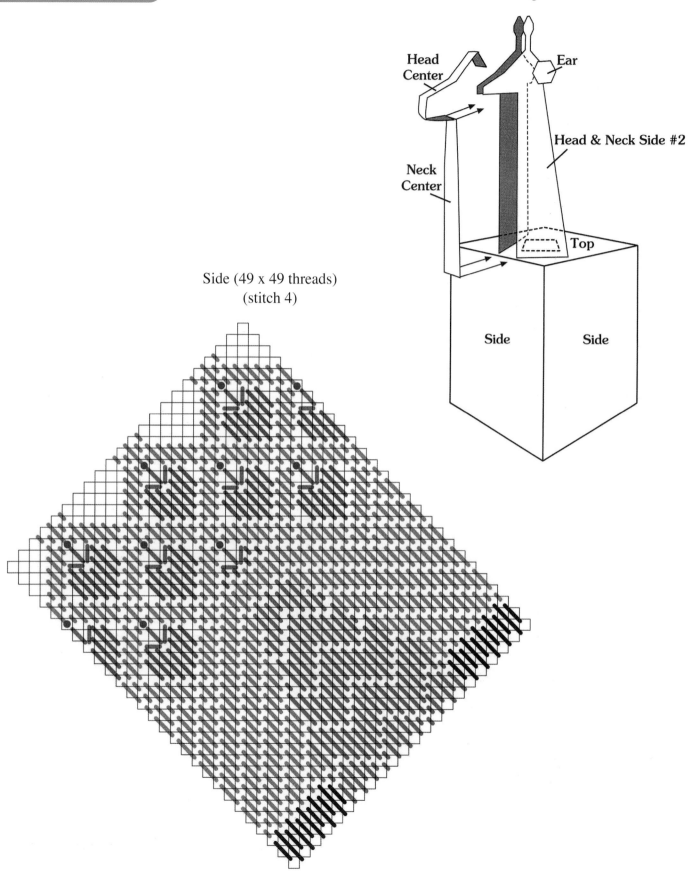

Head Center

Ear

Head & Neck Side #2

Neck Center

Top

Side   Side

Side (49 x 49 threads)
(stitch 4)

Flower
(8 x 8 threads)
(stitch 5)

Ear
(10 x 10 threads)
(stitch 2)

Head & Neck Side #1
(54 x 50 threads)

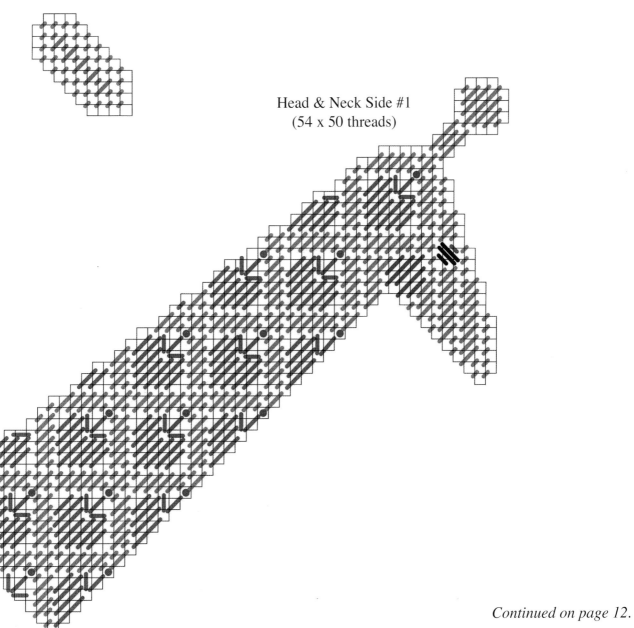

Continued on page 12.

Giraffe

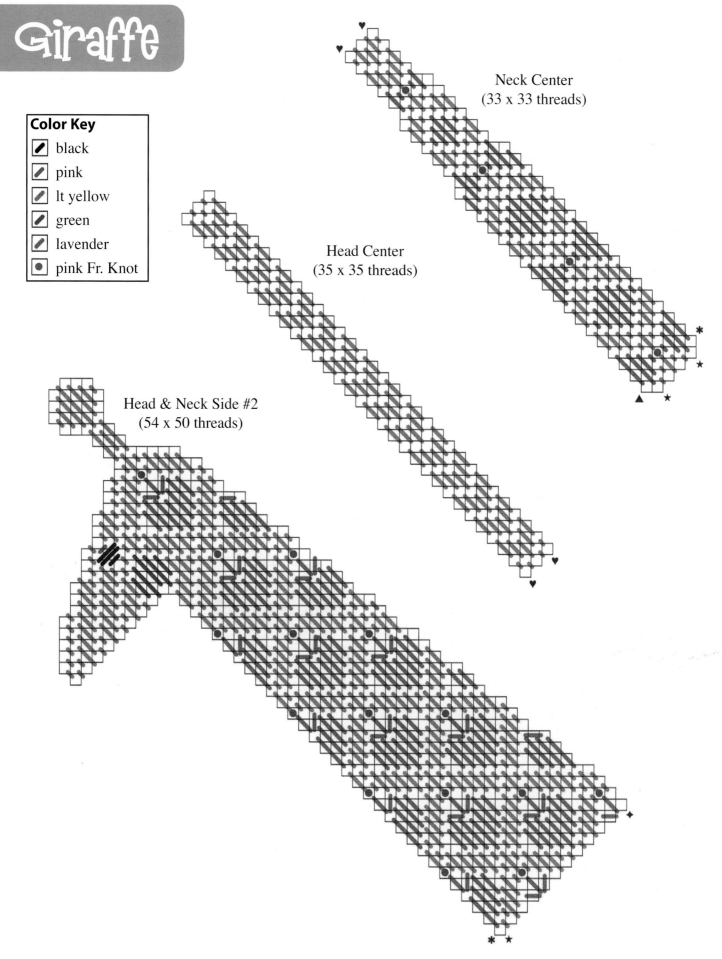

Color Key
- ✏ black
- ✏ pink
- ✏ lt yellow
- ✏ green
- ✏ lavender
- ● pink Fr. Knot

Neck Center
(33 x 33 threads)

Head Center
(35 x 35 threads)

Head & Neck Side #2
(54 x 50 threads)

12

Bunny

Shown on page 8.

Size
9"w x 12$\frac{1}{2}$"h x 7"d
(fits a 4$\frac{1}{4}$"w x 5$\frac{1}{4}$"h x 4$\frac{1}{4}$"d boutique tissue box)

Supplies
Three 10$\frac{1}{2}$" x 13$\frac{1}{2}$" sheets of 7 mesh plastic canvas
Worsted weight yarn
#16 tapestry needle
Ten $\frac{3}{4}$" pink pom-poms
One 1$\frac{1}{2}$" pink pom-pom
Nylon thread

Stitches Used
Backstitch, French Knot, Gobelin Stitch, Overcast
Stitch, Scotch Stitch, and Tent Stitch. Refer to **General
Instructions**, pages 36-39, for stitch diagrams.

Instructions
Follow charts to cut and stitch Bunny pieces, leaving
stitches in shaded areas unworked. Using pink Overcast
Stitches, cover unworked edges of Tongue and Inside
Ear pieces. Using ecru Overcast Stitches, cover
unworked edges of Muzzle and Foot pieces.

Matching ▲'s, use peach Overcast Stitches to join Hat
to Head. Match ♥'s and tack Tongue to Head. Using
ecru yarn, refer to photo to tack Muzzle to Head.
Using pink yarn, tack one $\frac{3}{4}$" pom-pom to head for
nose.Using pink yarn, match ✪'s and ♣'s and tack
Inside Ears to wrong side of Head. Matching ■'s, use
ecru Overcast Stitches to join sides of Head together,
forming a cylinder. Follow arrows to fold and join
inside edges of Head together.

Match ★'s and work stitches in blue shaded area to
join front of Head to back of Head. Matching ♦'s, use
ecru and refer to Assembly Diagram to tack Head to
Top. Place an 8" length of green yarn around bottom of
Head; tack in place.

Work stitches in yellow shaded area to join Sides
along long edges. Using peach Overcast Stitches, join
unworked edges of Top to Sides.

Using lt green yarn, match ♦'s to tack Hand #1 to
Bunny's right Side. Match ♣'s to tack Hand #2 to
opposite Side. Using nylon thread, refer to photo for
placement and tack Carrot to Hand #1, Tongue, and
Top. Tack each Foot to front of tissue box cover. Tack
one $\frac{3}{4}$" pom-pom to top of Hat. For tail, tack 1$\frac{1}{2}$"
pom-pom to back of tissue box cover. Tack remaining
$\frac{3}{4}$" pom-poms to corners and points of Top.

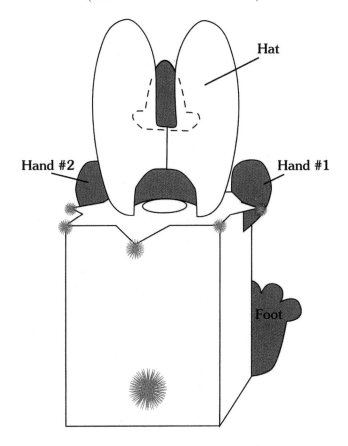

Assembly Diagram
(Note: Back view is shown.)

Continued on page 14.

Bunny

Color Key

✎	lt pink
✎	green
✎	lt green
✎	ecru
✎	lavender
✎	peach
⬤	black Fr. Knot
⬤	lavender Fr. Knot
⬤	peach Fr. Knot

Inside Ear (12 x 26 threads)
(stitch 2)

Hat (16 x 17 threads)

Head (67 x 47 threads)

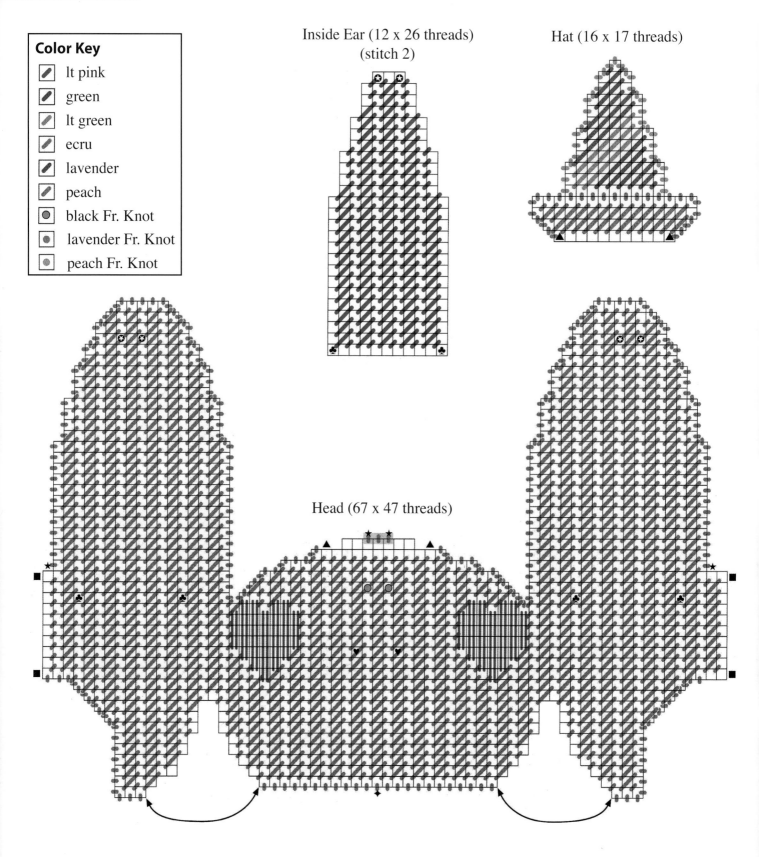

Hand #1 (17 x 17 threads)

Hand #2 (18 x 17 threads)

Tongue (6 x 6 threads)

Muzzle (12 x 6 threads)

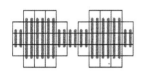

Side (32 x 38 threads)
(stitch 4)

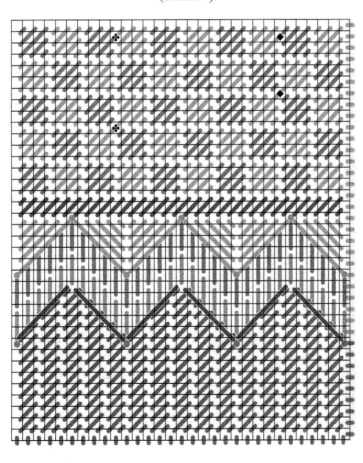

Continued on page 16.

Bunny

Carrot (23 x 23 threads)

Foot (22 x 29 threads)
(stitch 2)

Top (44 x 44 threads)

Color Key

- green
- lt green
- ecru
- lavender
- peach
- peach Fr. Knot

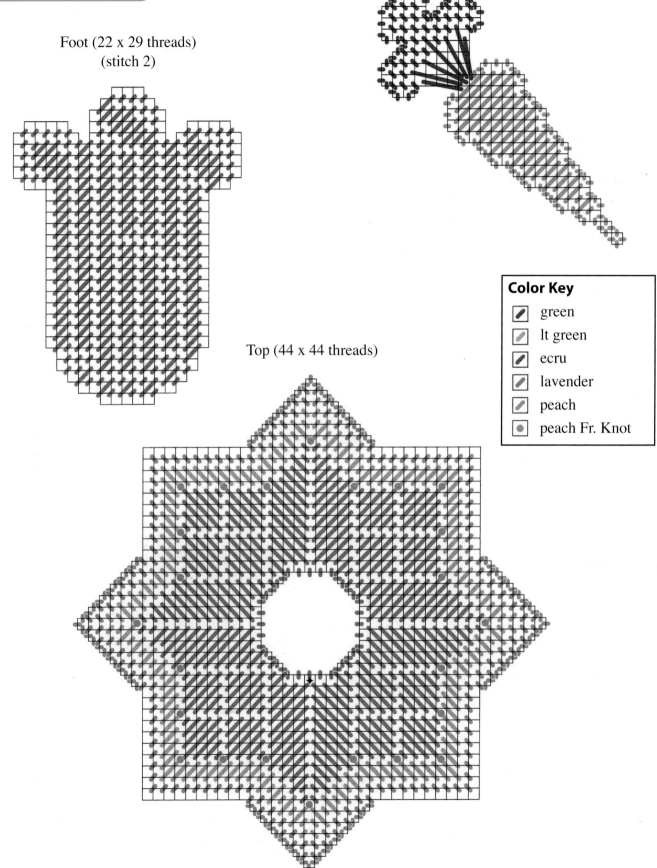

Peek·a·boo

Shown on page 8.

Size

4³/₄"w x 7¹/₂"h x 7"d
(fits a 4¹/₄"w x 5¹/₄"h x 4¹/₄"d boutique tissue box)

Supplies

Two 10¹/₂" x 13¹/₂" sheets of 7 mesh plastic canvas
Worsted weight yarn
Black embroidery floss
#16 tapestry needle
Fine-toothed comb

Stitches Used

Backstitch, Gobelin Stitch, Mosaic Stitch, Overcast
Stitch, Scotch Stitch, Tent Stitch, and Turkey Loop
Stitch. Refer to **General Instructions**, pages 36-39, for
stitch diagrams.

Instructions

Follow charts to cut and stitch Peek-a-boo pieces.
Using aqua Overcast Stitches, cover edges of Hands.
Matching ✳'s and ◆'s, tack Hands to Front. Matching
★'s and ♥'s, use orange Overcast Stitches to join Head
Back to Front and Top. Using aqua Overcast Stitches,
join Top to Front along remaining unworked edges.
Using aqua Overcast Stitches, join Front to Sides.
Using white Overcast Stitches, join Back to Sides along
long edges. Join Top to Back and Sides. For Bangs, trim
Turkey Loops to 1" long. Separate yarn into plies and
comb; trim to ³/₄" long.

Color Key

▨	white
▨	aqua
▨	yellow

Top (32 x 32 threads)

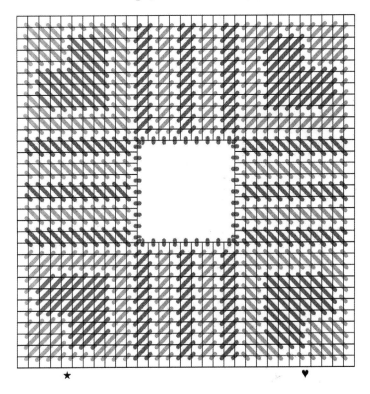

★   ♥

Side/Back (32 x 38 threads)
(stitch 3)

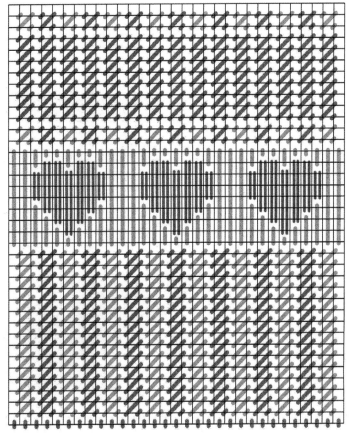

Continued on page 18.

Head Back (24 x 13 threads)

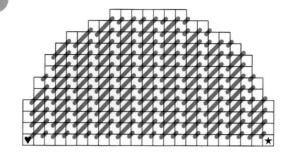

Hand #1 (15 x 24 threads)

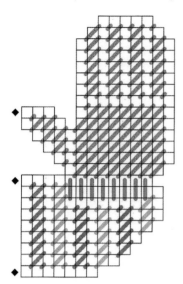

Hand #2 (15 x 24 threads)

Front (32 x 50 threads)

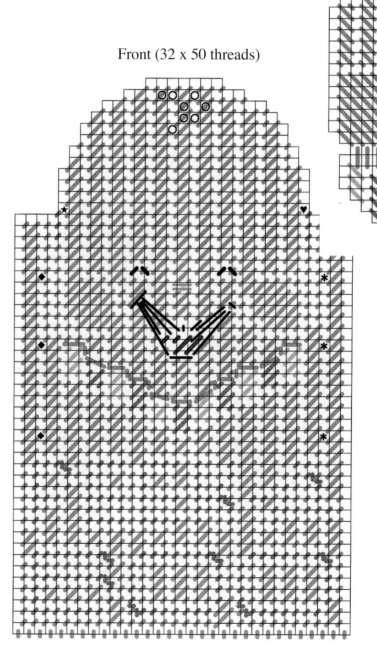

Color Key

✎	black
✎	pink
✎	orange
✎	white
✎	aqua
✎	dk orange
✎	flesh
✎	yellow
⊙	orange Turkey Loop
✎	black embroidery floss (use 6 strands)

Mini·Motifs

Shown on page 8.

Size

4³/₄"w x 5¹/₂"h x 4³/₄"d
(fits a 4¹/₄"w x 5¹/₄"h x 4¹/₄"d boutique tissue box)

Supplies

Two 10¹/₂" x 13¹/₂" sheets of 7 mesh
plastic canvas
Worsted weight yarn
#16 tapestry needle

Stitches Used

Backstitch, French Knot, Gobelin Stitch, Lazy Daisy
Stitch, Overcast Stitch, and Tent Stitch. Refer to
General Instructions, pages 36-39, for stitch diagrams.

Instructions

Follow charts to cut and stitch Mini-Motifs pieces.
Use yellow Overcast Stitches for all joining. Join
Sides along long edges, alternating Side #1 and Side
#2 pieces. Join Top to Sides. Using yellow Overcast
Stitches, cover unworked edges.

Top (32 x 32 threads)

Color Key
- ⊘ pink
- ⊘ lt green
- ⊘ lavender
- ⊘ yellow

Continued on page 20.

Mini·Motifs

Color Key

- ✎ black
- ✎ pink
- ✎ lt pink
- ✎ orange
- ✎ lt yellow
- ✎ green
- ✎ lt green
- ✎ blue
- ✎ white
- ✎ lavender
- ✎ aqua
- ✎ yellow
- ● black Fr. Knot (use 2-ply yarn)
- ⊘ black Lazy Daisy

Side #1 (32 x 38 threads) (stitch 2)

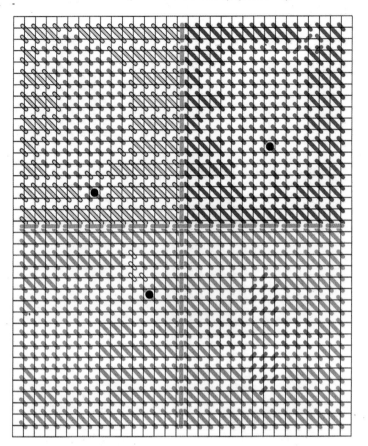

Side #2 (32 x 38 threads) (stitch 2)

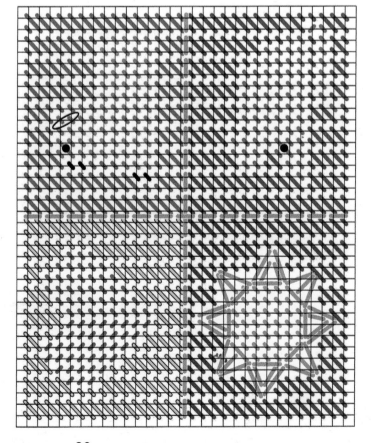

www.leisurearts.com

Friendly Bear set

switch Plate Cover

Large Flower
(6 x 6 threads) (stitch 2)

Nose
(12 x 12 threads)

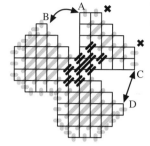

Shown on page 21.

Size

5¼"w x 6¾"h

Supplies

One 10½" x 13½" sheet of 7 mesh plastic canvas
Worsted weight yarn
#16 tapestry needle

Stitches Used

Backstitch, French Knot, Gobelin Stitch, Overcast Stitch, Reversed Tent Stitch, and Tent Stitch. Refer to **General Instructions**, pages 36-39, for stitch diagrams.

Instructions

Follow charts to cut and stitch Switch Plate Cover pieces. Matching A to B and C to D, fold down top section of Nose. Using lt tan Overcast Stitches, join these sections. Matching ✖'s, join top edge of Nose to Body along unworked threads. Tack each side of Nose to Body. Matching ★'s, join Left Arm to Body along unworked edges. Matching ♥'s, join Right Arm to Body along unworked edges. Following Diagram for placement of stitches, use lt tan to join Flowers to Switch Plate Cover.

Right Arm
(13 x 7 threads)

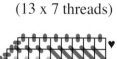

Left Arm
(13 x 7 threads)

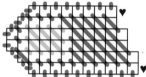

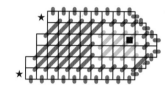

Body
(50 x 50 threads)

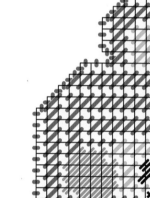

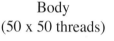

Color Key

⟋	white
⟋	lt pink
⟋	pink
⟋	aqua
⟋	green
⟋	lt tan
⟋	tan
⟋	black
●	white Fr. Knot

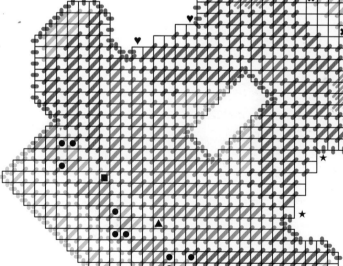

Small Flower
(4 x 4 threads) (stitch 2)

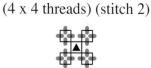

Diagram

Wall Hanging

Shown on page 21.

Size

5¼"w x 6¾"h

Supplies

Two 10½" x 13½" sheets of 7 mesh plastic canvas
Worsted weight yarn
#16 tapestry needle
Sawtooth hanger

Stitches Used

Backstitch, Gobelin Stitch, Overcast Stitch, Reversed Tent Stitch, and Tent Stitch. Refer to **General Instructions**, pages 36-39, for stitch diagrams.

Instructions

Follow charts to cut and stitch Wall Hanging pieces. Matching A to B and C to D, fold down top section of Nose. Using lt tan Overcast Stitches, join these sections. Matching ✖'s, join top edge of Nose to Body along unworked threads. Tack each side of Nose to Body. Matching ■'s, use tan Overcast Stitches to join Left Ear to Body along unworked edges. Matching ▲'s, join Right Ear to Body along unworked edges. Matching ◗'s, join Left Arm to Body along unworked edges. Matching ★'s, join Right Arm to Body along unworked edges. Matching ♠'s, use white Overcast Stitches to join Left Leg to Body along unworked edges. Matching ♦'s, join Right Leg to Body along unworked edges. For drawstring on each Leg, follow Diagram to weave white yarn back and forth across booties. Matching ♣'s, join Diaper to Body along unworked edges of Diaper. Using aqua Overcast Stitches, join Pin Head to Pin along unworked edges. To attach Pin to Diaper, match ♥'s and work three white Gobelin Stitches over Pin through Diaper and Body. Tack Wings to wrong side of Bee; tack Bee to Rattle. Tack Rattle to Right Arm. Securely attach hanger to wrong side of Body.

Color Key	
✎	white
✎	orange
✎	lt tan
✎	tan
✎	black

Bee Wing
(6 x 6 threads)
(stitch 2)

Bee (7 x 7 threads)

Right Arm (25 x 12 threads)

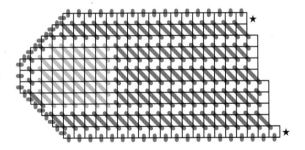

Left Arm (25 x 12 threads)

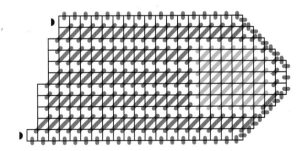

Continued on page 24.

Wall Hanging

Pin Head
(7 x 7 threads)

Pin
(15 x 15 threads)

Left Ear
(12 x 11 threads)

Right Ear
(12 x 11 threads)

Body
(60 x 60 threads)

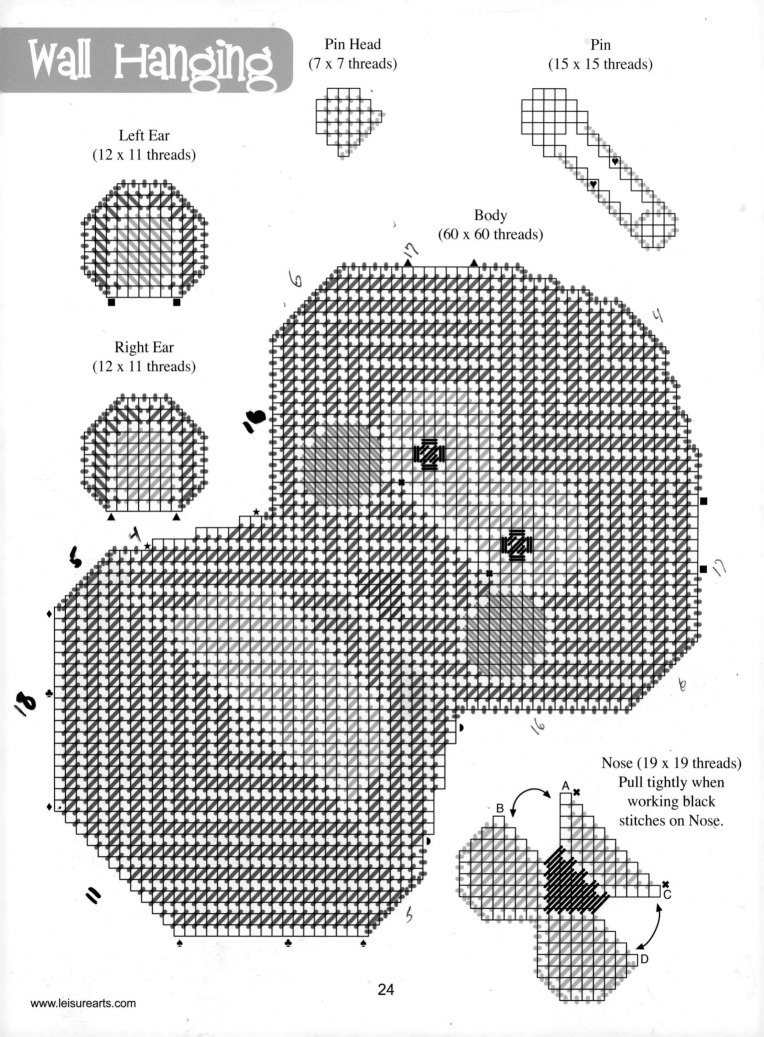

Nose (19 x 19 threads)
Pull tightly when
working black
stitches on Nose.

www.leisurearts.com

Color Key

white	
lt pink	
pink	
aqua	
lt tan	
tan	
black	

Diaper
(24 x 24 threads)

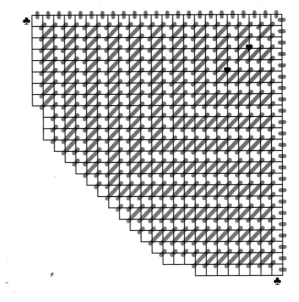

Rattle
(22 x 22 threads)

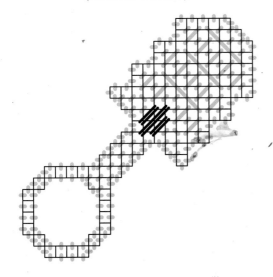

Left Leg
(32 x 19 threads)

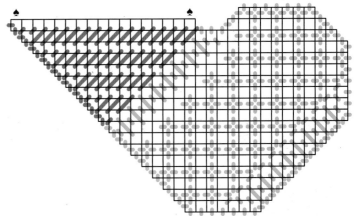

Right Leg
(32 x 19 threads)

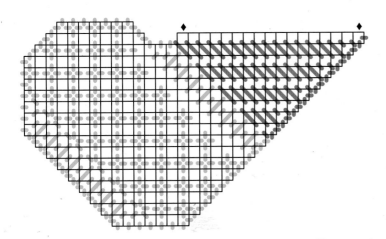

Diagram

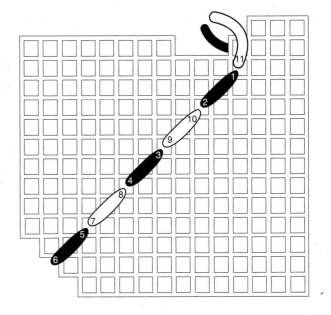

storage Box

Shown on page 21.

Size
3¼"w x 3¼"h x 3¼"d

Supplies
Two 10½" x 13½" sheets of 7 mesh plastic canvas
Worsted weight yarn
#16 tapestry needle

Stitches Used
Backstitch, Cross Stitch, Eyelet Stitch, French Knot, Gobelin Stitch, and Overcast Stitch. Refer to **General Instructions**, pages 36-39, for stitch diagrams.

Instructions
Follow charts to cut and stitch Box pieces. Using aqua Overcast Stitches, join Front and Back to Sides. Join Bottom to Front, Back, and Sides. Join Top to unworked edge of Back. Cover remaining unworked edges.

Color Key	
⟋	yellow
⟋	orange
⟋	lt pink
⟋	pink
⟋	purple
⟋	aqua
⟋	lt tan
⟋	tan
⟋	black
●	pink Fr. Knot
●	black Fr. Knot (use 2 plies)

Top/Bottom (22 x 22 threads) (cut 2) (stitch 1)

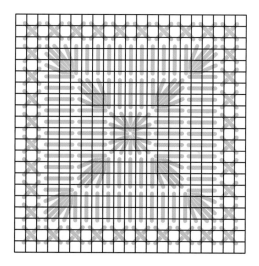

Front/Back/Side (22 x 22 threads) (stitch 4)
Complete background with yellow backstitches as indicated on chart.

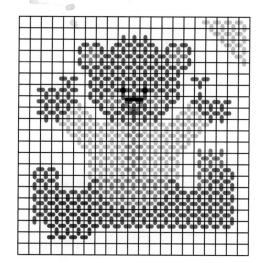

Teddy Basket

Teddy Basket

Size
5³/₄"w x 10"h x 10"d

Supplies
Four 10¹/₂" x 13¹/₂" sheets of 7 mesh plastic canvas
Worsted weight yarn
#16 tapestry needle
Clear-drying craft glue

Stitches Used
Backstitch, Cross Stitch, Gobelin Stitch, Overcast Stitch, Reversed Tent Stitch, and Tent Stitch. Refer to **General Instructions**, pages 36-39, for stitch diagrams.

Instructions
Follow charts to cut and stitch Basket pieces, working Backstitches last and leaving lavender shaded areas unworked. Glue Muzzle to Head Front. Matching ▲'s, use pink Overcast Stitches to join Hat Trim to Head Front. Repeat to join Hat Trim to Head Back. Matching ♥'s, join Collar to Head Front. Repeat to join Collar to Head Back. With wrong sides together, match ◆'s and use matching color Overcast Stitches to join Head Front to Head Back along unworked edges, leaving edges below ◆'s unworked.

Matching ★'s, place Handle Supports on wrong side of Side A and Side B. Work stitches in lavender shaded areas through two thicknesses of canvas to join Sides to Handle Supports. With wrong sides together, use yellow Overcast Stitches to join Handle pieces along long edges, leaving stitches between ■'s and ♣'s unworked. Matching ■'s and ♣'s, place Handle Supports between Handle pieces. Using yellow Overcast Stitches, work through three thicknesses of canvas to join Handle pieces to Handle Supports. Working through four thicknesses of canvas, join Handle pieces to Sides and Handle Supports.

Matching ♠'s, join Foreleg A to Side A. Matching ◗'s, join Foreleg B to Side B. Tack Cuffs to Forelegs and Sides. With wrong sides together, use aqua Overcast Stitches to join Wagon Handle Front to Wagon Handle Back, leaving stitches between ✖'s unworked. Matching ✖'s, join Wagon Handle to End along unworked edge of Wagon Handle. Tack Wagon Handle to End. Using matching color Overcast Stitches, join Sides to End.

Working through three thicknesses of canvas, use matching color Overcast Stitches to join Head Front and Head Back to Sides. Using lt green Overcast Stitches, join Basket Bottom to unworked edges of Basket. Glue Wheels to Sides.

Hat Trim
(18 x 5 threads) (stitch 2)

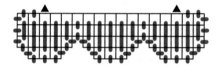

Collar
(24 x 6 threads) (stitch 2)

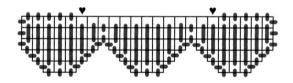

Wheel (14 x 14 threads)
(stitch 4)

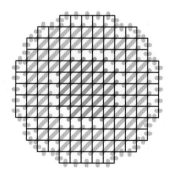

Muzzle (10 x 8 threads)

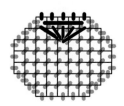

28

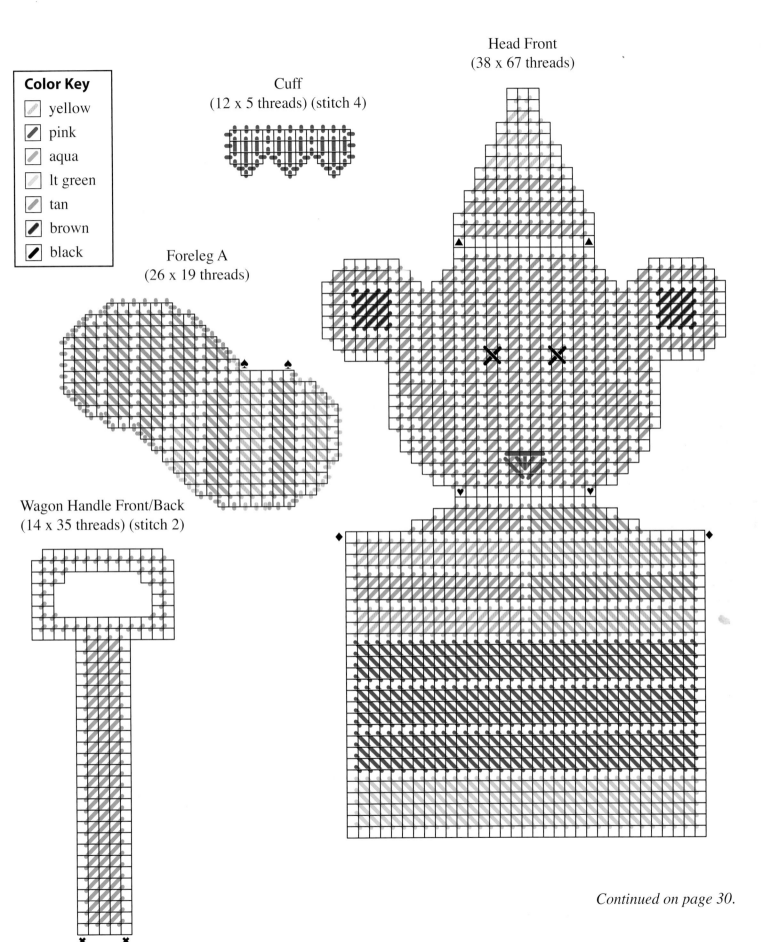

Color Key

▨	yellow
▰	pink
▨	aqua
▨	lt green
▨	tan
▰	brown
▰	black

Cuff
(12 x 5 threads) (stitch 4)

Head Front
(38 x 67 threads)

Foreleg A
(26 x 19 threads)

Wagon Handle Front/Back
(14 x 35 threads) (stitch 2)

Continued on page 30.

29

Teddy Basket

Head Back
(38 x 67 threads)

Color Key

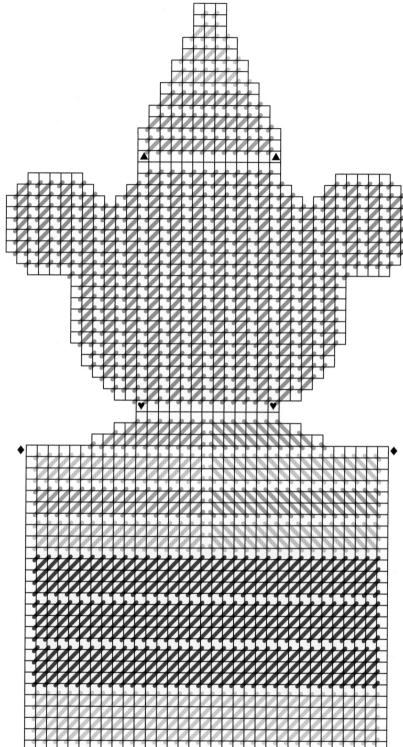

yellow

pink

aqua

lt green

tan

Foreleg B
(26 x 19 threads)

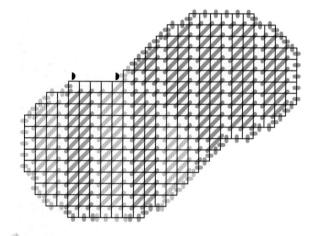

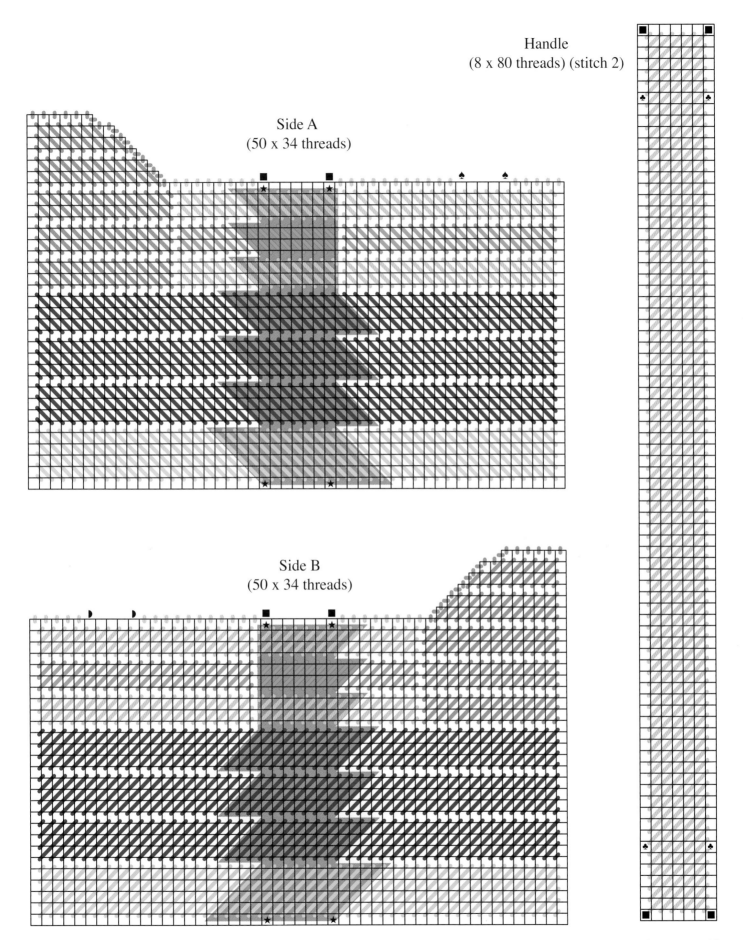

Handle
(8 x 80 threads) (stitch 2)

Side A
(50 x 34 threads)

Side B
(50 x 34 threads)

Continued on page 32.

Teddy Basket

Basket Bottom
(50 x 34 threads)

Color Key

▨	pink
▨	lt green
▨	tan

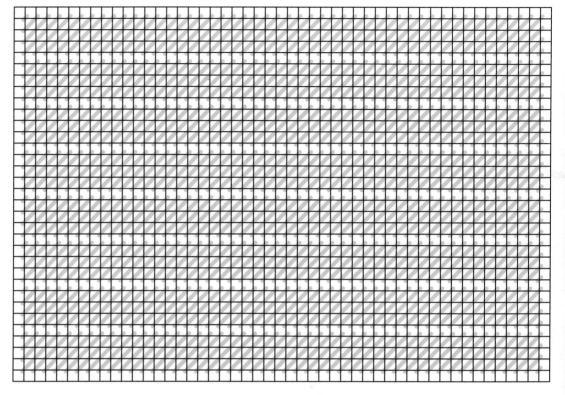

Handle Support
(8 x 35 threads) (cut 2)

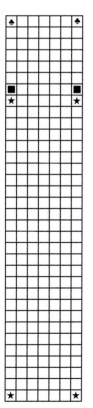

End
(34 x 34 threads)

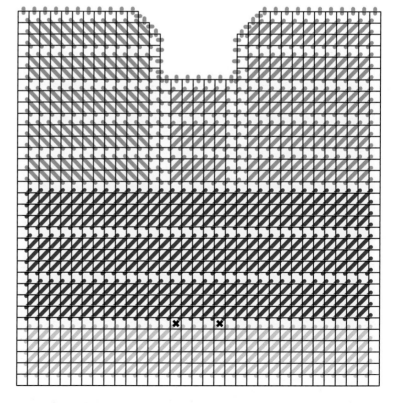

32

Baby shower

Supplies

One 10½" x 13½" sheet of 7 mesh plastic canvas
Worsted weight yarn
#16 tapestry needle
Clear-drying craft glue

Stitches Used

Backstitch, Cross Stitch, French Knot, Gobelin Stitch, Overcast Stitch, and Tent Stitch. Refer to **General Instructions**, pages 36-39, for stitch diagrams.

Color Key

white		green	
yellow		lt beige	
orange		brown	
flesh		black	
pink		● pink Fr. Knot	
lt blue		● black Fr. Knot	
lt green			

Cradle Nut Cup

Size

3"w x 2¼"h x 3"d

Instructions

Follow charts to cut and stitch Cradle Nut Cup pieces. Matching ★'s, use yellow to join corners of Bottom along unworked edges. Matching ♦'s, use yellow to join Bottom to Base along unworked threads. Thread 8" of green yarn through Top at ●'s; tie in a bow and trim ends. Referring to photo for placement, match **v**'s and use yellow to join Top to Bottom at **v**'s.

Cradle Nut Cup Base
(20 x 20 threads)

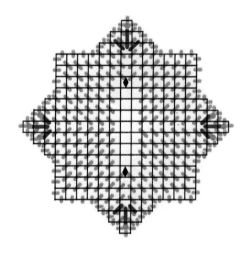

Cradle Nut Cup Bottom
(18 x 22 threads)

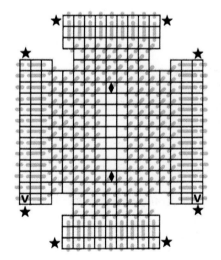

Cradle Nut Cup Top
(19 x 19 threads)

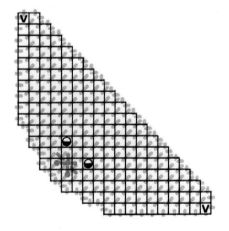

34

Bear Napkin Ring

Size

2¹⁄₂"w x 5"h

Instructions

Follow charts to cut and stitch Bear Napkin Ring pieces. Matching ★'s, use white to tack Diaper to Front at ★'s. Matching ✳'s, use yellow to join Back to Front along unworked edges.

Bear in Bootie
(18 x 21 threads)

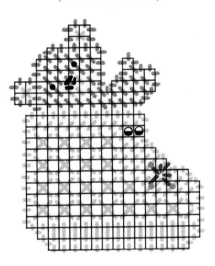

Bear Napkin Ring Back
(16 x 16 threads)

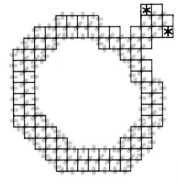

Bear Napkin
Ring Diaper
(8 x 8 threads)

Bear Napkin Ring Front
(29 x 29 threads)

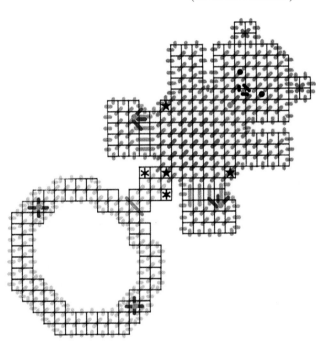

Additional Favors

Approx Size

3"w x 3¹⁄₄"h

Instructions

Follow charts to cut and stitch desired pieces. For Baby In Crescent Moon, match ▲'s and use white to join Arm to Baby. For Stork, match ✦'s and use white to join Stork Wing to Stork. Tie 12" of lt blue yarn in a bow around neck; trim ends. For Bear in Bootie, thread 8" of yellow yarn through canvas at ⬤'s; tie in a bow and trim ends.

Arm
(4 x 2 threads)

Stork
(21 x 24 threads)

Baby in Crescent Moon
(19 x 20 threads)

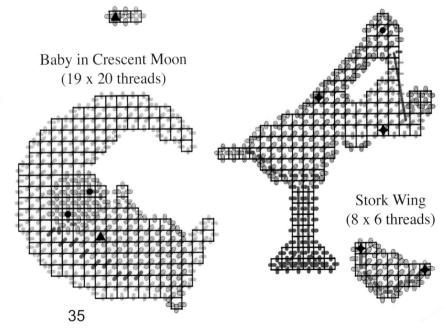

Stork Wing
(8 x 6 threads)

General Instructions

Working with Plastic Canvas

Counting Threads. The lines of the canvas are referred to as threads. Before cutting out the pieces, note the thread count of each chart listed above the chart, indicating the number of threads in the width and height. To cut plastic canvas pieces accurately, count **threads** (not **holes**) as shown in **Fig. 1**.

Fig. 1

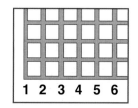

1 2 3 4 5 6

Marking the Canvas. You may use an overhead projector pen to mark the canvas. Outline shape with pen, cut out shape, and remove markings before stitching.

Cutting the Canvas. Cut as close to the thread as possible without cutting into the thread. If you don't cut close enough, "nubs" or "pickets" will be left on the edge. Make sure to cut all nubs from the canvas before stitching because nubs will snag the yarn and are difficult to cover. A craft knife is helpful when cutting a small area from the center of a larger piece of canvas. When using a craft knife, protect the table below with a layer of cardboard.

When cutting canvas along a diagonal, cut through the center of each intersection. This will leave enough plastic canvas on both sides of the cut so that both pieces may be used. Properly cut diagonal corners will be less likely to snag yarn and are easier to cover.

Working with Worsted Weight Yarn

Most brands have plies which are twisted together to form one strand. When the instructions indicate two plies of yarn, separate the strand of yarn and stitch using only two of the plies.

Reading the Color Key

A color key is included for each project, indicating the color used for each stitch on the chart. Additional information may also be included, such as the number of plies to use when working a particular stitch.

Reading the Chart

When possible, the drawing on the chart looks like the completed stitch. For example, the tent stitches on the chart are drawn diagonally across an intersection of threads just as they look on the piece. When a stitch cannot be clearly drawn on the chart, like a French Knot, a symbol will be used instead.

Stitching the Design

Securing the First and Last Stitches. Don't knot the end of your yarn before you begin stitching. Instead, begin each length of yarn by coming up from the wrong side of the canvas and leaving a 1"-2" tail on the wrong side. Hold this tail against the canvas and work the first few stitches over the tail. When secure, clip the tail close to the stitched piece. Long tails can become tangled in future stitches or can show through to the right side of the canvas. After all the stitches of one color in an area are complete, end by running the needle under several stitches on the back. Trim the end close to the stitched piece.

Using Even Tension. Keep your stitching tension consistent, with each stitch lying flat and even. Pulling or yanking the yarn causes the tension to be too tight, and you will be able to see through your project. If the tension is too loose, the stitches won't lie flat. Most stitches tend to twist yarn. Drop your needle and let the yarn untwist occasionally.

36

Joining Pieces

Straight Edges. To join two or more pieces along a straight edge, place one piece on top of the other with right or wrong sides together. Make sure the edges are even, then overcast the pieces together through all layers.

Shaded Areas. Shaded areas usually mean that all the stitches in that area are used to join pieces of canvas. Do not work these stitches until the project instructions say you should.

Tacking. To tack pieces, run your needle under the backs of some stitches on one stitched piece to secure the yarn. Then run the needle through the canvas or under stitches on the piece to be tacked in place. This should securely attach pieces without tacking stitches showing.

Uneven Edges. When you join a diagonal edge to a straight edge, the holes will not line up exactly. Keep the pieces even and stitch through the holes as many times as necessary to completely cover the canvas.

Stitch Diagrams

Unless otherwise indicated, bring needle up at 1 and all odd numbers and down at 2 and all even numbers.

Backstitch

This stitch is worked over completed stitches to outline or define **(Fig. 2)**. It is sometimes worked over more than one thread. It can also be used to cover canvas **(Fig. 3)**.

Fig. 2   **Fig. 3**

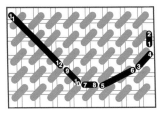   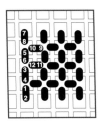

Cross Stitch

This stitch is composed of two stitches **(Fig. 4)**. Cross the top leg of each stitch in the same direction. The number of intersections may vary according to the chart.

Fig. 4

Diagonal Mosaic Stitch

A variation of the mosaic stitch, this stitch is worked in diagonal rows **(Fig. 5)**.

Fig. 5

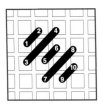

Eyelet Stitch

This stitch forms a square over four threads of canvas **(Fig. 6)**. It consists of 16 stitches worked in a clockwise fashion. Each stitch is worked from the outer edge into the same central hole.

Fig. 6

French Knot

Come up at 1. Wrap yarn once around needle. Insert the needle at 2 and pull it through the canvas, holding the yarn until it must be released **(Fig. 7)**.

Fig. 7

Gobelin Stitch

This straight stitch is worked over two or more threads or intersections **(Fig. 10)**. The number of threads or intersections may vary according to the chart.

Fig. 10

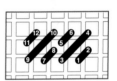

Lazy Daisy Stitch

Bring the needle up at 1, make a loop and go down at 1 again. Come up at 2, keeping yarn below needle **(Fig. 11)**. Pull needle through and secure loop by bringing yarn over loop and going down at 2.

Fig. 11

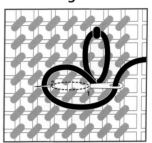

Mosaic Stitch

This three-stitch pattern forms small squares **(Fig. 12)**.

Fig. 12

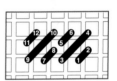

38

Overcast Stitch

This stitch covers the edge of canvas and joins pieces **(Fig. 13)**. It may be necessary to go through the same hole more than once to get even coverage on the edge, especially at the corners.

Fig. 13

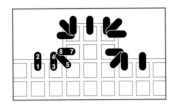

Scotch Stitch

This stitch may be worked over three or more threads and forms a square. **Fig. 14** shows a Scotch stitch worked over three threads.

Fig. 14

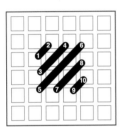

Tent Stitch

This stitch is worked in horizontal or vertical rows over one intersection **(Fig. 15)**. Refer to **Fig. 16** to work the reversed tent stitch.

Fig. 15

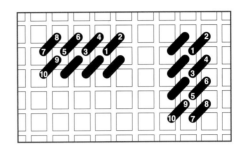

Fig. 16

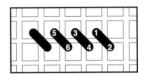

Turkey Loop Stitch

This stitch is composed of locked loops. Bring needle up through hole and back down through same hole, forming a loop on top of the canvas. Make a locking stitch across the thread directly below or to either side of the loop as shown in **Fig. 17**.

Fig. 17